3 Little Bones

ALSO BY THE AUTHOR

You Might Have to Audition to Iron My Shirts:
A Single Mom's Search for Love
with Annie Brady

3 Little Bones

A Guide to Seafood Processor Jobs in Alaska

Diane Brady

Library of Congress Control Number: 2026902918

ISBN: 979-8-218-93080-6

Author's Disclaimer: No companies I applied to, was hired by or worked for are identified.

Cover photo by Dustin Safranek (iStock gallery)

Sockeye Salmon Illustration by bazzier (iStock gallery)

Alaska Map by Borhan Uddin (iStock gallery)

Interior photos by Diane Brady

Author photo by Angelica Bianca Zeta

Printed in the United States of America

Durango, Colorado

For Roger Miller

You make my dreams come true....

Contents

Preface

I started the journey into the Alaska seafood processing industry almost fifty years ago. At age 23, I was looking for a "working adventure" that would yield enough money to travel and support my outdoors lifestyle. While living in the Seattle area, at that time, I talked with a friend whose brother had worked in the Aleutian Islands as a processor and asked many questions. Armed with enough information to sound informed about the industry, I boldly walked into the employment office at the same company in late June 1976, to discuss work in Alaska. Although the interaction went well, I was uncertain if my application would be considered and what the time frame for working would be.

A few days later, I received a phone call from the company. "We'd like to hire you," they said. "It's a six-month contract. Can you leave in two days?"

I was shocked! Two days? I didn't own the required work clothes and gear. I didn't know where I could purchase everything quickly. And six months put me away from home during the holidays. Since I was in a relationship that probably would not last a long separation, I realized the timing of this "working adventure" was all wrong. Reluctantly, I declined the opportunity. However, the "spark" had been lit, even if briefly, and working in remote Alaska as a seafood processor was to become a vision I carried for many, many years.

In 2015, after having lived in Alaska for eighteen years, moved to Denver, Colorado to raise a daughter as a single mom, served in the U.S. Peace Corps and settled in the foothills above Denver in a long-term, stable relationship, I decided to revisit the seafood processor dream — this time I wanted to earn money to buy an airplane — and, consequently, applied to a position in the Aleutians East Borough.

This was Pre-Covid, and the hiring process required submitting an application online, attending an in-person orientation, which included watching a video about the company and nature of the work, interviewing with a recruiter and getting questions answered before a job offer was issued. Not realizing how competitive seafood processor jobs were, I opted to drive to Oklahoma for the orientation in late May, rather than going to Seattle (main office) a month earlier. That decision cost me more than the driving time and travel expenses. By delaying the hiring process, I was placed on a waiting list for my desired location. Again, the six-month contract, if not started soon, would put me away from home during the holidays. More importantly, though, I had already purchased a ski pass in Colorado and did not want to lose valuable time using it. I called the company, asked for an update on a possible departure date, but decided to withdraw my application. Although I wanted to earn the money for an airplane, I considered my overall quality of life more important, at that time.

In 2024, while working on the Trail Safety Team at Telluride Ski & Golf Resort, I decided the timing was right to apply for a seafood processor job in Alaska. This time, however, I decided to work during the shorter B season and the summer Bristol Bay salmon run, rather than commit to six months. If I survived the experience, I could always pursue a longer contract during the winter A season.

I researched companies and applied to one that seemed the most suitable. Since I submitted my application just after the processor job posted in February, I immediately received an email request for an interview. That was accomplished quickly, and soon I was exchanging emails with the recruiter to answer various questions and complete the onboarding process. I was all set this time and started gathering the clothing and gear I wanted to take to Alaska.

Less than two months later, however, I learned the company I expected to work for, starting in June, had been purchased by a larger company. The recruiter sent an email saying if we wanted to work we had to submit a new application and start all over again. So, I did what was suggested, attended a Zoom informational meeting with the new company but never heard back regarding my application. Since I was determined to actually work as a seafood processor that summer, I did more research and contacted a smaller company. Their processing model was innovative, and I appreciated their new approach. I applied, was hired, completed onboarding and was waiting for my travel itinerary and airline ticket to be emailed. And then, disaster struck!

On May 13, 2024, I was diagnosed with melanoma. The cancer originated in a mole on my upper arm that had been present all of my life. Due to unexpected stress from my mother's death the year before and subsequent issues with my siblings regarding the estate, the mole began to change. Although I had decided to deal with it after the Alaska job, at my daughter's request I had it biopsied in early May.

Once diagnosed, dealing with the medical issue immediately was critical. I knew several months of work stress, lack of sleep and a questionable diet would not help the situation. Reluctantly, I bailed again. The gal I had been working with at the company was disappointed I would not be joining them. However, she understood the situation and assured me I could work the following year.

My journey to eradicate the melanoma completely and return to robust health is one for the record books, but will not be covered in this publication. In the future, I may write a short book about the alternative medical protocols I used successfully. It is my sincere belief that had I listened to my

doctors, who only suggested the standard cancer protocol —
surgery, radiation and chemotherapy — I would either be in
hospice care now or dead.

In the fall of 2024, when the melanoma was no longer
a limiting factor in my life, I revisited the seafood processor plan. And, although I wanted to reapply to work at the
company that had hired me several months before, I didn't
want to wait until their seasonal jobs posted and, instead,
researched other companies with earlier hiring dates.

I considered a small company in the Bristol Bay area of
Alaska that I had read about before. This time, I submitted an
application the same day the processor job posted. In less than
two weeks, I was interviewing with a recruiter by phone. After
he spoke with my primary reference, I was offered a contract
and completed all of the paperwork as quickly as possible.
Forty-nine years after first embarking on this journey, I was
ready and eager to go.

I successfully completed my contract during the summer of
2025 and earned a lot of money in thirty-four days. Most of
the time, I stood in one place along the fillet production line
from noon until 4:30 a.m. — a 16-hour shift. The work, as
expected, was cold, wet and slimy. My back hurt, my feet and
legs became swollen and several fingers were numb from the
repetitive motions. But, I was focused on the goal — earning
money to build an Experimental, Light-Sport Aircraft — and
determined to survive to the end. As a 72-year-old, I watched

processors a third of my age complain and quit. Some were fired. Others could not mentally and physically manage the work environment and stress. Fortunately, I was surrounded by many happy, upbeat people of all nationalities and ages, who kept me laughing and smiling. "If SHE can do this," they often said, pointing to me on the line, "then YOU can do this." I believe I served as an inspiration to others during my season in Naknek, Alaska. And I hope that inspiration is carried forth to future workers, at that location.

I am not an expert on seafood processing. However, after researching the industry and applying multiple times over several decades — and having been hired, onboarded by different companies and worked an entire season at one facility — I have a good understanding of the hiring process and nature of the work, in general.

It is my sincere hope that *3 Little Bones — A Guide to Seafood Processor Jobs in Alaska* — helps the curious applicant looking for a "working adventure" in remote Alaska find a suitable company or more for possible employment. Being a Seafood Processor — even for one season — is an experience you will share throughout your lifetime. Be proud of your perseverance and ability to achieve financial and personal goals. You are a Rock Star!

Prologue

3 **<u>Little Bones</u>** — the bones in the neck of a sockeye salmon, attaching the fish head to the body. As a seafood processor in the Fillet department, during the 2025 summer Bristol Bay salmon season in Naknek, Alaska, one of my department Leads regularly said, "Three Little Bones." While on the production line, I always made an effort to locate and remove them with wide tweezers. It was a satisfying moment, when I was able to grasp and extract them smoothly.

1 Introduction

Life as a seafood processor in remote Alaska should be considered a "working adventure." The experience will be different for everyone and is influenced by your overall attitude about living and working in an environment that is challenging both physically and mentally. You will meet people from around the world and be expected to work well together as a dynamic team. Maintaining a good sense of humor, being flexible with the work assignment and willing to take on additional responsibilities are all valuable attributes that will help you thrive in the workplace.

Before you apply for this "working adventure," establish clear goals and understand your motivation to perform such tedious work. Whether those goals are financial, professional, experience-oriented or something else, keeping them in mind throughout the season will help you successfully complete the contract. At the end, you will walk away with a renewed understanding of your personal limits and pride in your accomplishment.

There are different seasons, when seafood processing takes place in a variety of locations around Alaska. The starting and ending dates vary by region and the type of fish harvested. Some companies operate year round. In general, A season is during the winter months into the spring, and B season can be in the summer into the fall. The salmon season is the largest around the state, primarily during the summer, and is usually the shortest — one to three months in duration. It's a great option for college students, teachers and those who want to earn a significant amount of money in a concentrated period of time. In addition, working an entry-level position during the salmon season is a good introduction to the seafood industry, without signing a contract for six months.

Seafood processing companies come and go. Even the most long-term, established operators experience financial difficulties, especially if the fish runs are limited. They may survive lean times or be sold to another company. Make sure the companies you apply to are still actually in business or, instead, operating under a different name. Some companies are under a larger parent company, although they operate independently. During the application process, for example, you may be asked if you will allow your application to be shared with a sister company. Keep all of your options open for employment.

Within the seafood industry, you could work in a shore-based plant, on an at-sea processor or on a floating processor. What employment arrangement best interests you should be considered when seeking job opportunities. Company websites usually provide a clear explanation of their operation and a detailed seafood processor job description. Regardless of the type of operation involved, research each company thoroughly.

The number of hours you will work per day/week vary, depending upon the quantity of harvested fish entering the plant. Shifts of 12, 14 or 16 hours are common. Overtime pay of 1.5 times the hourly wage, after eight hours, adds up quickly. The working conditions in seafood processing plants differ, depending upon which department you are assigned to. Some are pleasantly warm and don't involve much contact with raw fish. Others are cold, wet, slimy and bloody. You could be working in the Fish House, Fillet, Packaging, Roe, Shipping or Cannery. The work is tedious, and you are unlikely to have a choice on where you start in production. However, if the conditions are too difficult for you to manage and you are a dedicated employee, you can certainly ask to be moved. Depending upon the employer and their needs elsewhere, that might be arranged. There are no guarantees, however. You will be hired to do the job of a seafood processor, and that can be in any department, performing any task, after orientation and training.

Housing and living situations vary, too, depending upon where you are stationed. Expect to share a room with at least one other person or a group in a dormitory of bunk beds. Individual space may be extremely crowded on a vessel or more expansive if shore-based. Roommates may work different shifts, which requires everyone to be quiet and mindful of those sleeping. Restrooms and shower facilities are also shared. At most companies, personal laundry is done for you weekly. Meals and snacks are available either at designated times in the mess hall or continuously. There is always plenty of food to fuel hungry, tired seafood processors.

After completing the application process, being offered a contract, signing and submitting all of the onboarding documents and preparing for your "working adventure," you will eventually receive a travel itinerary with airline reservations to the work site. Some companies will fly you from airports close to home, while others will only provide transportation from Seattle, Washington or Anchorage, Alaska. If you successfully complete the contract, transportation costs to and from Alaska are usually covered. However, if you quit early or are fired, you will be responsible for those expenses. The same applies to room and board. Some companies charge a daily fee, if you work more than eight hours in a day. Others include housing and food. This is also something to consider, when researching potential employers.

The more you learn and understand about a particular seafood processing company before making a commitment, the more confident and satisfied you will be, when you arrive in Alaska. There should be few surprises. Most companies want their new hires to be as informed as possible and may provide online Zoom sessions with the Human Resources staff to answer questions, prior to the season.

<u>KEY POINTS</u>

- Consider employment as a seafood processor a "working adventure."

- Maintain a good attitude, sense of humor and be flexible with your assignment.

- Set clear goals and understand your motivation to perform the work.

- Determine which season, duration and type of processing operation is best for you.

- Overtime hours at 1.5 times the hourly wage add up quickly.

- Working conditions and assignments vary, and you usually do not have a choice in task.

- Housing is shared with one or more roommates on different shifts.

- Plentiful meals and snacks may be available continuously or during designated times.

- Transportation, housing and food costs may be fully covered by the company or not.

- Being informed and prepared for the position will help you be confident and satisfied.

Fins: A Funny Moment

One morning on the fillet production line, I noticed the fillets coming out of the deboning machine had fins still attached to the edges. At the time, we did not have a worker with a sharp knife stationed down the line, to trim the fillets, again, before they were sorted and sent to Packaging. I stepped away from my position and walked a short distance to talk to one of the processors trimming fillets, before they were sent through the deboning machine.

"You've got to cut off the fins," I said.

"I am. It's the guy next to me," he replied.

I returned to my position along the conveyor belt and continued picking bones out of sockeye salmon fillets. Several hours later, the fillets were still coming through with the fins attached. It was frustrating, because I wanted the product to look presentable, and all I had in my hand was a pair of wide tweezers.

I walked over to the same processor I had talked to earlier.

"You've got to cut off the fins," I said.

This time, his face lit up with a beautiful grin. "Just bite them off."

We both couldn't stop laughing!

2
Seafood Processing Overview

More than 100 years ago, Alaskan Natives harvested, processed and traded seafood with other tribes. The first commercial cannery started in 1878. Since those times, the industry in Alaska has grown and is considered the leading manufacturer in the state.

<u>CERTIFIED FISHERIES IN ALASKA</u>

- Alaska Black Cod (Sable Fish)

- Alaska Cod

- Alaska Crab

- Alaska Flatfish

- Alaska Halibut

- Alaska Pollock

- Alaska Rockfish and Atka Mackerel

- Alaska Salmon

- Alaska Herring (Under assessment as of May 2025)

Commercial fishing and processing take place in multiple regions in the state. From the protected waters of Southeast Alaska to the treacherous open waters of the Bering Sea, adventurous fishermen and dedicated laborers endure difficult conditions — both mental and physical — to help keep the industry alive. Alaska seafood products are shipped and enjoyed all around the world.

Ironically, due to the seasonality of the work, relatively low hourly wages, remote locations, housing challenges, low status and other factors, most employers seek a work force of nonresidents from outside of Alaska. It is not unusual to hear multiple languages spoken along the production line in a busy seafood processing plant.

What attracts people willing to work long, hard hours in difficult conditions? For most, it is the opportunity to make a substantial amount of money in a short period of time.

Overtime pay is at 1.5 times the hourly wage, which adds up quickly during long shifts. The job might be a one-time experience or something to do for several seasons, to reach a financial or career goal. Some folks return year after year and move to different positions within a particular company. And some, over time, have gone from being an entry-level processor to the President or CEO. The possibilities are unlimited for those willing to work hard, take direction and learn new skills.

After an introduction to the seafood industry in Alaska, those with an entrepreneurial vision might work directly on the sea as a crewmember aboard a fishing boat and, eventually, purchase their own craft. Work onboard a vessel is more dangerous, and the financial rewards unpredictable. However, the opportunity to take home a percentage of the catch and earn far more than a land-based seafood processor is attractive.

KEY POINTS

- Seafood processing started in Alaska more than 100 years ago.

- There are many Certified Fisheries in the state.

- Alaska seafood harvesting and processing take place in multiple regions along the coast.

- Most employees in the industry are not residents of Alaska.

- There are opportunities to earn a lot of money, with overtime at 1.5 times the hourly wage.

- Opportunities to work different positions within a company or move up the ladder in seniority are available to those willing to work hard, take direction and learn new skills.

- Those with an entrepreneurial vision often work on a fishing boat and, eventually, operate their own vessel.

Map of Alaska

ALEUTIAN ISLANDS CHAIN AND WESTERN COASTLINE

CENTRAL AND SOUTHEAST ALASKA

3
Companies Hiring Seafood Processors

The following companies are listed in alphabetical order. They may process only one kind of fish during a specific period of time, in one region, or operate during A or B season or year round, in multiple regions and process a variety of products. Some of the larger companies own shore-based production facilities in more than one location. Others hire seafood processors to live and work on vessels, while in the fishing grounds — at-sea processors. And several more have floating processors, where a large ship or barge receives harvested fish.

When considering a particular company, review the main website thoroughly. Learn as much as you can about their operations. The knowledge you gain first will help you be more selective when choosing where to submit applications. Use the employment link provided to reach the opportunities and job openings pages. Please note that most websites have a contact form, which allows you to send a message. And don't forget — a phone call can save you a lot of time waiting for a reply.

ALASKA GENERAL SEAFOODS

- **https://www.akgen.com**

- **https://www.akgen.com/employment**

- P.O. Box 1359, Edmonds, WA 98020-1359

- 130 2nd Ave. S., Edmonds, WA 98020

- (425) 485-7755

ALASKA GLACIER SEAFOODS, INC.

- **https://www.alaskaglacierseafoods.com**

- **https://www.alaskaglacierseafoods.com/employment**

- P.O. Box 34363, Juneau, AK 99803

- 13555 Glacier Hwy., Juneau, AK 99801

- (907) 790-3590

- EMAIL: info@alaskaglacierseafoods.com

<u>ALASKA PACIFIC SEAFOODS (NORTH PACIFIC SEAFOODS)</u>

- **<u>https://www.northpacificseafoods.com/alaska-pacific-seafoods.html</u>**

- **<u>https://www.northpacificseafoods.com/jobs--trabajos.html</u>**

- 130 2nd Ave. S., Edmonds, WA 98020

- (206) 726-9900

<u>ALASKA SEAFOOD COMPANY</u>

- **<u>https://alaskaseafoodcompany.com</u>**

- **<u>https://tlingitandhaida.gov/careers/? career c ategories=alaska-seafood- company#search</u>**

- 5731 Concrete Way, Juneau, AK 99801

- (800) 451-1400

<u>ALASKAN LEADER FISHERIES</u>

- **https://alaskanleader.com**

- **https://alaskanleader.com/careers**

- 8874 Bender Rd., Ste. 201, Lynden, WA 98264

- (360) 318-1280

<u>AMERICAN SEAFOODS</u>

- **https://www.americanseafoods.com**

- **https://www.americanseafoods.com/jobs/vessels-crew-jobs**

- Market Place Tower, 2025 First Ave., Ste. 900, Seattle, WA 98121

- (206) 448-0300

ARCTIC STORM MANAGEMENT GROUP, LLC

- **https://www.arcticstorm.com**

- **https://www.arcticstorm.com/employment**

- 2727 Alaskan Way, Pier 69, Seattle, WA 98121

- (800) 929-0908

- (206) 547-6557

- EMAIL: recruiter@arcticstorm.com

BRISTOL WAVE

- **https://bristolwaveseafoods.com/**

- **https://bristolwaveseafoods.com/commericial-fishing-jobs/**

- 641 West Ewing St., Seattle, WA 98119

- (206) 284-1162

- EMAIL: hr@bristolwaveseafoods.com

<u>CIRCLE SEAFOODS</u>

- **<u>https://circleseafoods.com</u>**

- **<u>https://circleseafoods.com/careers</u>**

- 408 West Curtis St., Aberdeen, WA 98520

- (360) 209-7719

<u>COASTAL VILLAGES</u>

- **<u>https://coastalvillages.org</u>**

- **<u>https://coastalvillages.org/job-openings</u>**

- 1801 Fairview Ave. E, Ste. 300, Seattle, WA 98102

- (206) 436-0604

<u>COPPER RIVER SEAFOODS</u>

- **<u>https://www.copperriverseafoods.com</u>**

- **<u>https://www.copperriverseafoods.com/join-our-team</u>**

- 1400 E, 1st Ave., Anchorage, AK 99501

- (907) 522-7806

<u>E.C. PHILLIPS AND SON</u>

- **<u>https://ecphillipsalaska.com</u>**

- **<u>https://ecphillipsalaska.com/apply-now</u>**

- 1775 Tongass Ave., Ketchikan, AK 99901

- (907) 247-7975

- (907) 247-7492 (Main — other locations)

- <u>EMAIL</u>: info@ecpalaska.com

<u>E & E FOODS, INC.</u>

- **<u>https://eefoods.com</u>**

- **<u>https://eefoods.com/page/employment</u>**

- 900 Powell Ave. SW, Renton, WA 98057

- (206) 768-8979

GLACIER FISH COMPANY

- **http://www.glacierfish.com**

- **https://glacierfishcareers.multiscreensite.com**

- 2001 West Garfield St., Terminal 91, Bldg. A-1, C-107, Seattle, WA 98119

- (206) 298-1200

- EMAIL: info@glacierfish.com

GOLDEN ALASKA SEAFOODS

- **https://www.goldenalaska.com**

- **https://www.goldenalaska.com/jobs**

- (206) 441-1990

- EMAIL: joes@goldenalaska.com

ICY STRAITS SEAFOODS

- **https://www.icystraitseafoods.com**

- 2825 Roeder Ave., Bellingham, WA 98225

- (360) 734-8175

<u>LEADER CREEK FISHERIES</u>

- **<u>https://www.leadercreekfisheries.com/</u>**

- **<u>https://www.leadercreekfisheries.com/employ ment</u>**

- P.O. Box 1359, Edmonds, WA 98020-1359

- 130 2nd Ave. S, Edmonds, WA 98020

- (206) 547-6900

- <u>EMAIL</u>: info@leadercreek.com

<u>NORTHLINE SEAFOODS</u>

- **<u>https://www.northlineseafoods.com</u>**

- **<u>https://www.northlineseafoods.com/careers</u>**

- P.O. Box 5487, Bellingham, WA 98225

- (907) 747-4755

- <u>EMAIL</u>: info@northlineseafoods.com

<u>OBI SEAFOODS</u>

- **<u>https://www.oceanbeauty.com</u>**

- **<u>https://www.oceanbeauty.com/careers</u>**

- 600 Powell Ave. SW, Renton, WA 98057

- (206) 284-6700

- <u>EMAIL</u>: info@oceanbeauty.com

<u>PACIFIC SEAFOOD</u>

- **<u>https://www.pacificseafood.com</u>**

- **<u>https://careers.pacificseafood.com</u>**

- 16797 SE 130th Ave. Clackamas, OR 97015

- (503) 905-4427

- <u>EMAIL</u>: recruiting@pacificseafood.com

ROGUE WAVE PROCESSING

- **https://www.roguewaveprocessing.com**

- **https://www.roguewaveprocessing.com/#employment**

- 38664 Kalifornsky Beach Rd., (Mile 14.5), Kenai, AK 99611

- (907) 531-4155

SEAFOODS PRODUCERS COOPERATIVE

- **https://www.spcsales.com**

- **https://www.spcsales.com/employment**

- 507 Katlian St., Sitka, AK 99835

- (907) 747-5811

SILVER BAY SEAFOODS, LLC

- **https://www.silverbayseafoods.com**

- **https://careers.silverbayseafoods.com/**

- 4019 21st Ave. W, Ste 300, Seattle, WA 98199

- (206) 960-4140

- <u>EMAIL</u>: information@silverbayseafoods.com

SIXTY NORTH SEAFOODS

- **https://www.sixtynorthseafoods.com**

- **https://www.sixtynorthseafoods.com/apply**

- 210 Jim Poor Ave., P.O. Box 239, Cordova, AK 99574

- (907) 424-7755

<u>TRIDENT SEAFOODS CORPORATION</u>

- **<u>https://www.tridentseafoods.com</u>**

- **<u>https://www.tridentseafoods.com/join-our-team</u>**

- 5303 Shilshole Ave. NW, Seattle, WA 98107

- (800) 367-6065

- (206) 789-8545

- <u>EMAIL</u>:humanresources@tridentseafoods.com

<u>UNISEA</u>

- **<u>https://www.unisea.com</u>**

- **<u>https://www.unisea.com/join-our-team/</u>**

- 15400 NE 90th St., Redmond, WA 98052

- (425) 881-8181

- <u>EMAIL:</u> info@unisea.com

UNITED STATES SEAFOODS

- **https://www.unitedstatesseafoods.com**

- **https://www.unitedstatesseafoods.com/ussemp loyment**

- 1801 Fairview Ave. E, Ste 100, Seattle, WA 98102

- (206) 763-3133

WESTWARD SEAFOODS, INC.

- **https://www.westwardseafoods.com**

- **https://recruiting2.ultipro.com/WES1015WS EA/JobBoard/233903b4-7e86-45c7-a7dc-4eb7 1cebcfb3/?q=&o=postedDateDesc**

- 3015 112th Ave. NE, Ste 100, Bellevue, WA 98004

- (206) 682-5949

- <u>EMAIL</u>: contact@wsi.us

Restroom Break: A Funny Moment

After wasting almost all of my valuable "snack break" in the restroom line outside of the plant, I started doing what everyone else did — take a quick bathroom break during my shift. The process was not simple. First, I noted the time on the big clock in the Fillet department. Then, I walked quickly but carefully through the Fish House, over slippery floors, to the Gear Room. Next, I rinsed my plastic smock and rubber boots using a sprayer hose attached to the wall, removed my gloves and sleeves, placing them into the proper containers or trash can, hung up my wet smock on a designated hook, removed my protective head cover and, then, washed and dried my hands. At that point, I could exit the plant and use a restroom.

One day, the Housekeeping staff was busy cleaning the small, three-stall bathroom. I could not use the space. However, there were two portable restrooms available on the deck, so I entered one. The door latch seemed strange, but I managed to lock it. A few moments later, I tried to open the door. I turned the knob *this way and that. I pushed on the door. No matter what I tried, it would not budge. Yikes! I was locked into the tiny stall!*

I started to bang the door and shout for anyone in the area. A guy in the adjacent portable restroom heard me. In order to explain how to unlock the door, he went back inside to lock and unlock the unit. Then he talked me through the process, which was not intuitive at all, and I finally emerged from captivity. I felt stupid for having gotten stuck in the restroom, until the guy confessed it had happened to him the day before! Later, I learned several others had experienced the same situation.

Before returning to the Fillet department, I put on all of my PPE (Personal Protective Equipment) again, carefully hustled over the slippery floor and entered my assigned work area. I approached the Supervisor and confessed I had tried to make a fast turnaround — eight minutes was my record — but had gotten locked into the portable bathroom. She smiled. It seemed obvious she had heard the same true story before. After that, I only took a break outside of the Housekeeping staff's restroom cleaning schedule!

4
Hiring Window and Competitive Industry

Each company operating during either A or B season, or both, has its own hiring window. Those open year round may consider applications continuously. Most are looking for potential seafood processors many months before the season begins. Companies also like to rehire former employees and will either contact them directly before the position posts for the general public or indicate on the employment page that only former employees can apply, at that time. Those who worked hard under difficult conditions, maintained a good attitude about their assignments, were flexible and willing to move to other departments in the plant, as needed, and expressed a desire to return are considered first.

If you do not have seafood processor experience, do not worry. Companies expect to hire many new, entry-level workers each year. Some folks return season after season and move up in rank to become Leads, Supervisors or higher.

Everyone starts at the bottom as a seafood processor, unless they are applying for a highly skilled position — electrician, maintenance technician for specific equipment, etc. Other positions in the company are usually hired from within. Returners can let their employer know they are interested in working in a different department, either during the application and rehire process or once arriving at the facility. The company may need help in Quality Assurance, Security, Safety, Gear Room, Food Service, Laundry, Housekeeping or other areas that support production.

How do you know when the hiring window is for a specific company? You don't! The fastest way to determine when you should be vigilant, and check their website daily for open positions, is to call them. Ask to speak to someone in the Human Resources department, if available. Regardless, most who answer the phone can provide a general time frame of when seasonal hiring begins.

Keep a notebook, especially if you call and speak to a company representative. Record the date of the call, the person's name and position, any pertinent information gathered and, of course, when you can expect to see applications accepted online. Your notebook is a valuable resource and should be consulted, when selecting which company or more to apply to.

Seafood processor jobs are highly competitive. People from countries all over the world seek employment in the industry. Living and working in remote Alaska is a big draw, especially when you realize prior experience is not required and substantial amounts of money can be earned. For those reasons, the sooner you get an application into the system, the better your chances of being hired. Although a company may continue to accept applications right up to the start or even during the operating season, those who do not act quickly are often placed on a waiting list.

If you are on a waiting list for a particular company, there is no guarantee you will be able to work for them that season. However, if you can be flexible in your life situation and are willing to leave home quickly, if contacted, you may still get a position.

Why is it worth being patient? Not everyone a company hires as a seafood processor is suited for the work. Although company websites usually provide detailed job descriptions, many applicants do not seriously consider what they are signing up for. As mentioned in the Introduction, the long hours, cold and wet environment, and the overall nature of life on a production line, cause many people to give up and go home either early in the season or at some point during the season. If production is of relatively short duration, that seafood processor may not be replaced. Personal injury or a health issue, that cannot be managed while working, may cause someone to leave. Workers can be fired, too, for failing to report to their assigned shift on time or for other reasons.

KEY POINTS

- Call targeted companies to ascertain the hiring window and gather pertinent information.

- Keep a notebook of companies you contacted and the information gathered.

- Check company websites regularly, particularly when close to the application period.

- Be one of the first people to apply for a seafood processor position.

- If placed on a waiting list, be available to travel to Alaska quickly, if the company contacts you.

Fillet Jam: A Funny Moment

*M*ost days, I positioned myself next to a deboning machine on the conveyor line. Regularly, I opened the protective flap and carefully removed excess bones that had accumulated. Sometimes, another processor or maintenance worker sprayed the equipment with water, clearing out any debris that inhibited action of the machine. Even when we tried diligently to keep everything clear, fillets got jammed into the unit. A thick fillet might cause a big jam of fish from moving smoothly from one side of the conveyor to the other.

Although I tried to glance at the deboning machine frequently, there were times when I did not see the mess quickly. A gal who often worked across from me was a bit farther away and at the right angle to peer under the basket-like mechanism that pulled the bones out.

"Hey," she shouted, pointing to the jam of fillets. I'd spring into action, pulling a fish or several out or reaching into the side area to free what was stuck. Then, I'd grab a plastic tray, and *everyone on the line quickly placed fillets into it, so they could be run through the machine again.*

I loved working with this gal! She was so animated, when she shouted to get my attention. I'll never forget her pointing and shouting, "Hey!"

5
Researching the Culture of a Company

Every company has its own unique culture. The overall working environment a seafood processor experiences — from shared housing, food selections, variety of departments for assignment to recreational activities available when there is down time off the production line — influences an individual's viewpoint. One employee may embrace the job opportunity and thrive, while another may hate every aspect of it and, consequently, not make it to the end of the season.

If you know someone you trust and respect who worked as a seafood processor somewhere, ask that person for an honest review of life and work at that particular company. It's not uncommon to find friends referring friends, husbands with experience encouraging their wives to work a season or two and even parents introducing their children to the industry. Friends planning to work during the same season often request to be housed together.

When sharing your interest in employment as a seafood processor in Alaska, you may meet people who worked for multiple companies in a variety of locations. Ask them what they liked and didn't like about their experiences at each company. Do they have any advice that could be helpful to you, when selecting a company to apply to or not?

There are several online job sites, videos and forums that publish reviews of seafood processor jobs, in general, and positions at specific companies. Spend the time to research and read what is available. Again, realize these are the opinions of strangers. In the end, you must make your own decisions about what company or more to apply to.

WEBSITES FOR JOB REVIEW RESEARCH

- **https://www.indeed.com**

- **https://www.glassdoor.com**

- **https://www.reddit.com**

- **https://app.joinhandshake.com**

- **https://www.youtube.com**

- **https://www.salary.com**

- **https://www.facebook.com**

KEY POINTS

- Every company has a unique culture.

- Ask those you trust and respect, who worked in the industry, for their honest review.

- Talk to others about your interest in seafood processing and possibly meet someone who can offer advice.

- Conduct online research at many job sites, to obtain reviews of the work and companies.

Mud: A Funny Moment

Towards the end of my time in Naknek, Alaska, when the sockeye salmon run slowed in Bristol Bay, most seafood processors worked fewer hours. It was a welcomed break from my 16-hour shift — noon to 4:30 a.m. each day.

One afternoon, another worker in the Fillet department and I walked down the hill from the dormitory to explore the river and beach. A few guys were gathering dry wood and grass to start a bonfire, that evening. With camera in hand, I took photos of gulls flying over the water and fishing boats floating by. Slowly, I advanced closer to the river. The mud became thicker and thicker. Eventually, I was immobilized and could not free myself!

I started to shout for my co-worker, but he was farther down the beach. The guys gathering wood came to my rescue. However, they started pulling my arm at an awkward angle. I could not maintain my balance and realized I would soon be swimming in mud. Fortunately, I didn't wallow for long or get my rain pants and jacket too dirty, when I fell to my knees.

After getting enough beach and river experience for one day, I thanked my rescuers, waved to my friend and walked back up the hill. There was a large rain puddle near the dormitory. I took the opportunity to wash off some of the mud, but not until I took a photo of the muddy boots! Before entering my building, I removed the boots and immediately took them to the shower room. By the time they were clean, I had made a big mess in one shower stall. I grabbed a handful of paper towels from the dispenser, ran the shower and then got onto my hands and knees to clean the stall. Upon returning to my room, I removed my rain pants and jacket and returned to the restroom to rinse them in warm water. Fortunately, my rain gear was dry by the next day.

6
Application
Process

The application process begins with gathering information about a particular company online, reading reviews from current and former employees and asking yourself if this potential employer is the right fit for you. With so many companies hiring seafood processors, there are many options available.

You may want to consider obtaining a position during the summer salmon or B season, first. The commitment is usually for only one to three months, ending when the fish stop running or the fisheries period officially ends. The situation will allow you to evaluate work as a seafood processor without signing a contract for six months. If the experience meets your expectations and you want to continue employment in the industry, then apply for a winter A season job and/or consider returning to the original company the following year. As a returner, you may receive a small increase in the hourly wage, if you have already accrued many hours working for them, and also have the opportunity to switch departments, too.

Before Covid, many large seafood processing companies scheduled in-person hiring events in locations around the United States. Applicants were required to attend an in-person orientation to the seafood industry and learn specifics about that particular company. Often the CEO or another high-ranking employee of the company narrated a video introduction and tour of their Alaska facility. The video showed workers on various production lines in different departments, housing accommodations, mess hall, lounges and available recreational activities. Those conducting the orientation stressed the difficulty of the work and emphasized the seriousness of the commitment, once hired. Obviously, their goal was to employ seafood processors who would meet the company's needs and complete the contract successfully. After the presentation, those who had already submitted an application online were interviewed.

The application process became less complicated during and after Covid. Now, those interested in employment submit an application online. Sometimes, the company is part of a parent group, and you may be asked if you would like your application to be considered at a sister company, too. If recruiters, working with the Human Resources department, deem your application favorably, they will contact you and schedule an interview. It may be a group Zoom meeting or a personal call. Regardless, the recruiter will ask questions to ascertain your understanding of the nature of the work, ability to perform required tasks and how you will manage the tedious workday. They want to make sure you are well informed before continuing the hiring process. Towards the end of the interview, you will have the opportunity to ask questions. If you have already carefully reviewed the company's website, including the detailed job description, limited packing list and other information pertaining to the remote location, then your questions should focus on details not already provided or to clarify particular topics.

The application may ask you to provide job references. Some companies require the recruiter to speak with a reference, before officially making an offer and emailing you a contract to sign. Speak to your primary reference about your interest in work as a seafood processor and alert them that they may be called by a company representative.

Contracts vary in the amount of information they contain. Some are short letters, while others can be several pages long. However, they all contain your job title — Seafood Processor — and the hourly wage. The contract will also stipulate the employment as *"At Will."* That means either you, the seafood processor, or the company can terminate the relationship at any time, with or without notice or cause. Read and understand the contract thoroughly, before signing the document.

Depending upon the company, and the time interval before the season begins, you will receive, via email, multiple documents to fill out and sign online. This is the onboarding process and must be completed before the company can arrange your paid transportation to their Alaska facility. Onboarding documents usually include forms for personal and emergency contact information, a Health Questionnaire, Background Check Authorization, Form I-9 Employment Eligibility Verification and Form W-4 Employee's Withholding Certificate. If you want Direct Deposit of your paycheck into a specific bank account, you will provide the Routing Number.

Those who complete onboarding quickly will be booked on some of the first flights. Of course, returning seafood processors will usually be sent to Alaska earlier than new hires. However, if you are going to work during the shorter summer salmon or B season, getting to the plant and starting the job as soon as possible will yield more money earned, by the end of the season.

While waiting for that coveted travel itinerary to arrive via email, you should be gathering the proper clothes and supplies to make it through the entire season, as comfortably as possible. Consult the recommended packing list provided by the company. Consider revisiting the job reviews you already read before applying. Many will discuss "extras" to bring that were not listed. You can also read packing lists on other company websites. Some are more comprehensive than others. Regardless, this is the time to compile the items you will need, as you cannot rely on access to retail stores in the remote community or a reliable Internet connection for online purchases. Although many plants have a small company store, the hours it operates may not be convenient, or visiting it may cut into your limited "break time." Bring an adequate supply of any prescription medications and over-the-counter cold and flu products.

Aside from preparing the gear to pack, consider preparing your body. The work will most likely take its toll on you, at some point during the season. Arrive in Alaska fit and strong. Strive for optimum health and be well-rested before the trip north.

When traveling to Alaska, follow the guidelines provided by the company and on the itinerary. Label and take photos of each bag you are traveling with, in case luggage is delayed or lost. Include a legible paper inside each bag near the top, with your final destination and contact information. Realize you will probably pay baggage fees on multiple flights. The stopover in Anchorage may be long. This helps you make that last flight to your final destination, especially if you experienced flight delays en route.

<u>KEY POINTS</u>

- Gather information about the company or companies you want to apply to.

- Look at online employee reviews, again, to verify the company is right for you.

- Consider first applying to the shorter salmon or B season for summer work.

- Alert your primary reference about a possible call from a seafood company recruiter.

- Read and understand the contract before signing.

- Complete all onboarding paperwork quickly.

- Using the packing list, compile all of the items you will need in Alaska.

- Prepare your body with adequate rest for optimum health before the season begins.

- Label and take photos of all bags you are traveling with.

- Be ready to pay baggage fees on multiple flights to reach your destination and when returning home.

- Expect a possible long layover in Anchorage, Alaska.

Slow Dancing: A Funny Moment

The company I worked for during the summer of 2025 had a Spotify playlist that employees could contribute to before traveling to Alaska. I had added about sixty songs but only heard a handful of them, while on the production line. The music played 24/7 while the plant was operating. All genres were represented.

One evening after the dinner break, our shift returned to the department for another eight hours. Almost immediately, upon our arrival, the classic song by the Temptations — My Girl — blasted through the large speakers. Everyone started singing and swaying back and forth. A shared sense of comradery enveloped the room.

A tall gal from Argentina on the line behind me, tapped me on the shoulder. She smiled and held out her arms, inviting me to slow dance to the music with her. Although she spoke little English, we enjoyed a moment of friendship in that cold, wet room of fish fillets. It kept me smiling for hours.

7
Suggested Questions to Research

Moving to remote Alaska to work long hours as a seafood processor, in challenging conditions, generates many questions. The *"Careers"* or *"Join Our Team"* or *"Employment"* pages on most websites provide answers to a variety of general questions. If the answers to your specific questions are not available online or need clarification, write the questions in your notebook and be prepared to ask them during your interview. If you are not able to get everything answered, consider calling the Human Resources department at the company you are either applying to or have already been hired by. As mentioned several times in this Guide, your employer wants to be assured you arrive with a clear understanding of the work and living environment, in addition to the items you need to pack for the entire season in Alaska.

<u>HOUSING</u>

- Is room and board included without charge? Or is there a daily charge, if we work more than eight hours in a day? What is that daily charge?

- Do returners get free room and board? If yes, how many years of work are required to get that perk?

- What are the rooms like? Bunk beds? Twin beds?

- Will we have adequate storage or dressers for clothes and personal items?

- Do we need to bring our own sheets, blankets, pillow and a sleeping bag?

- Do the rooms have lockers and locks for our valuables?

- How many people to a room?

- May we request to room with a friend or a group of friends?

- Are all roommates working the same hours?

- Are there quiet hours in housing, if everyone works different shifts?

- How far away are the restrooms and shower facilities?

- How often are the restrooms closed for cleaning?

- Is there a lounge or recreational area to use when not working?

- Are there books, board games and a TV available in the lounge?

- Is Wi-Fi available? How reliable is the Internet connection?

- Do cell phones work? Which carriers are the most reliable in that region of Alaska?

- How far away is the company facility from a small town, retail and grocery stores?

- Is there a company store on site?

- What items are available to purchase in the company store?

<u>LAUNDRY</u>

- How do we do our laundry? Will it be done for us?

- How often is the laundry done? How many days of clothes will we need to bring?

- Is there an additional cost for our laundry to be done?

<u>WORK ENVIRONMENT</u>

- What is the hourly wage?

- What is the overtime wage?

- What are the work shifts and the hours they begin and end?

- May we choose which shift to work? Or are we assigned a shift for the entire season?

- How many days each week are we required to work?

- Are there many days without any work at all?

- May we choose which department to work in as a seafood processor in the production facility?

- If we have a difficult time with the assigned work, could we be moved to a different department or a different task in the same department?

- What work gear (PPE — Personal Protective Equipment) does the company provide?

- Can we wear our own gear instead of the company gear?

- Are personal lockers available to access during a break near the production facility?

- How many work breaks do we get during a shift? How long are the breaks?

- May we use a restroom between official breaks only or during a shift?

MEALS

- How long is the meal break? Must we clock out and in for the meal?

- Is the food in the mess hall self-serve, buffet-style? Or must we stand in line to be served by the kitchen staff?

- Are vegan and vegetarian options available during each meal?

- Are there vending machines to buy snacks?

SICKNESS OR INJURY

- What kind of medical office does the company maintain?

- Is there a doctor or nurse on duty 24/7?

- Is there a team of medical professionals who can respond to an emergency in the plant?

- Is there an Automatic External Defibrillator (AED) on site?

- Is there a hospital or clinic in the community near the plant?

- Is there a dentist in the area?

- Are there any pharmacies in the area?

- What over-the-counter or prescription medications are available in the company's medical office?

- How much prescription medication should I bring?

- Can we renew a prescription in the local town?

- If we get sick, must we continue working or may we take a day or more off?

- What medical situations require the company to send a seafood processor home?

- Who pays for the transportation if too sick or injured to work?

TRAVEL TO ALASKA

- Where is the Point of Hire for transportation to Alaska?

- Do you fly seafood processors from airports close to their homes?

- How much luggage should we bring?

- Are there baggage and weight limits on the commuter airlines servicing the region near the company facility?

- What happens if our luggage with work clothes is delayed or lost?

- Is there a Lost and Found or supply of used work clothes available if bags do not arrive?

<u>WILDLIFE</u>

- Is there dangerous wildlife in the area? Grizzly or black bears? Mountain lions? Moose? Other animals?

- What steps does the company take to keep employees safe, if wildlife wander near the facility?

- Is bear spray available to rent or purchase at the company store or at local retailers?

Where Art Thou? A Funny Moment

I loved the Fillet department, mostly because of the wonderful people I worked beside and the spontaneous craziness of the crew. Although I was sent briefly to the warm, dry packaging area, it was too quiet and civilized. Upon my return to Fillet the next day, one of my Leads greeted me with, "Welcome back!"

There was a group of young guys on different shifts who kept the entire room awake and engaged. Although I was never quite sure what triggered the actions, all of a sudden, people were banging metal objects — most likely fillet knives and wide tweezers — to music or just for kicks. My first impression was of being in a prison movie, where one guy bangs a metal cup on a bar and the next guy bangs something else. As the month progressed, a variety of animal sounds emerged from the group. It sounded like a Zoo! Between the noise of equipment used in the department, people speaking in many languages and the *loud music, there was always something going on to keep you awake.*

One day, a maintenance worker was standing beside me, troubleshooting an issue with the deboning machine and conveyor belt. He was a quiet guy and diligently made adjustments. All of a sudden, the room erupted with banging, singing, monkey sounds and general craziness. I don't know what specifically triggered the group, but as the commotion got louder, I started to laugh. When the maintenance worker finished the adjustments, I said, "I don't know if I'm in a Zoo or an Insane Asylum." The guy smiled. "I think it's a little of both."

8
Suggested Packing List

After being hired as a seafood processor and preparing to travel to remote Alaska for work, always consult the company website and available materials from the Human Resources department, as to what to bring. Remember that your employer wants you to have the best chance to succeed and be a productive member of their team. If you arrive at their facility with the proper gear — personal and work — and with a flexible, *"can do"* attitude, everyone will be happy.

Be aware of baggage weight and number restrictions and be prepared to pay extra fees. Although the goal is to bring what you expect to use, you do not want to leave behind items you may need. If in doubt, ask Human Resources for advice; they have dealt with all sorts of situations and can help guide you to make good choices.

As soon as you are officially hired and have a tentative departure date, begin organizing and gathering everything. This may require making purchases online or searching local thrift stores. Realize that you will be working in a cold, wet and messy environment, so bring used clothing you can leave behind or don't mind ruining.

In most locations, Internet and Wi-Fi access are limited or not available at the company site. Although there can be some down time, depending upon the fish run, you are more likely to be working, eating and sleeping, with little extra time for anything else. For that reason, think carefully about transporting valuable electronic devices. You do not want them damaged or stolen. Cell phone service may also be limited or unavailable. While traveling, though, you should have Internet connections at the airports.

REQUIRED WORK AND TRAVEL DOCUMENTS

- At least 2 forms of ID to comply with the I-9 Work Authorization Documentation.

- Real ID required by the airlines for travel.

- Debit or credit card to pay for baggage fees, unplanned overnight expenses and food.

- Cash to pay for food and snacks in the airports.

WORK GEAR

- Work clothes to last at least 7 days. Laundry is usually done for you once a week.

- Work clothes include: regular underwear, enough socks (wool or warm synthetic) to possibly change one or two times daily, compression knee-high socks or medical-grade compression leggings (almost everyone experiences swelling in their feet, ankles and legs), old t-shirts, turtle necks, sweatshirts and sweat-pants, long underwear tops and bottoms, fleece or flannel shirts, insulated pants, jeans, etc.

- Hats, neck gaiters, head bands and ties for long hair, baseball caps, gloves.

- Lightweight rain gear to wear under the required protective gear. (I found that by wearing my own comfortable, inexpensive rain gear over my warm clothes, I did not get as dirty each day and could wear the same clothes for more than one day. It was one of the best investments I made.)

- If you own comfortable XtraTuf Rubber boots (especially if yours are insulated), consider bringing them. Most companies provide rubber boots and may sell them to you at a discount. But if you already own something that works for you, consider bringing them (you can wear the boots while traveling and pack smaller, comfortable shoes for around the campus).

OTHER PERSONAL CLOTHES AND ITEMS

- Shower shoes (flip flops or Crocs).

- PJs or sleeping clothes you can wear in the common hallways to and from the restroom and shower facilities.

- Warm jacket and rain gear for travel and exploring, outside of the Alaska facility.

- A battery operated alarm clock or two. (I placed one alarm clock next to me in the bed but also had another one on the dresser, set for 5 minutes later. With only a few hours of sleep each day, getting out of bed can be difficult. If you are late, you can be fired!)

- A sleeping bag or extra blanket to supplement what is usually provided.

TOILETRIES AND PRESCRIPTION MEDICATIONS

- Bring enough prescription medications to get you through at least three months (obviously, more if under a six-month contract). Having extra is best. Cost of replacements is high or unavailable. Transport these items in your carry-on bag.

- Be conservative and smart with toiletry usage. Bar soap, for example, can be used for shampoo, if necessary. Bring a toothbrush, toothpaste, deodorant, shampoo, conditioner, shaving items, hairbrush, comb, face brush, feminine hygiene items, small pocket mirror, foot powder or spray. If you use a particular item at home, regularly, and do not want to be without it while in Alaska, pack it.

- Towels — washcloth, hand and shower. Shower caddy or bag to transport items to the public restroom facilities.

HEALTH AND WELLNESS ITEMS

- Assorted vitamins and supplements you take at home on a regular basis to keep your immune system functioning well. Your body will be stressed from hours of hard work and lack of sleep. Give yourself every advantage you can.

- Emergen-C packets, cold medications, cough drops, pain medications, hydration packs.

- Heating pad, leg massage exercise roller, knee and back braces, boot insoles, hand and toe warmers, boot dryer.

- Sleeping mask, ear plugs, small travel pillow.

- Water bottle (a collapsible bottle, that fits in a jacket pocket, is most convenient).

MISCELLANEOUS ITEMS

- Cell phone, phone charger, multi-outlet power strip, headphones or ear buds, laptop or tablet.

- Camera (if not using phone camera exclusively).

- Books, magazines, deck of cards, travel games, journal, notepads, pens, Post-it Notes.

- Extra prescription or reading eye glasses.

Di, Di, Di: A Funny Moment

*S*tanding in one place on a production line for 16 hours each day definitely takes a toll on the body. Even those much younger than me experienced swelling in their feet, ankles, knees and legs. Many complained of back pain. Fingers became numb from holding tweezers in the cold room, and repetitive motions caused discomfort in the hands.

I tried to get a little exercise each hour and would often march in place or move as if on a stair stepper machine to the beat of a song. I'd stretch my back, especially if there was a pause in the fillets coming down the conveyor. Basically, I tried whatever exercise I could to keep the blood and lymph circulating, particularly in my legs.

One evening after dinner — as we began our last eight hours on the line — a Michael Jackson song started playing — Billie Jean. I was already trying to move my legs, so the upbeat dance tune got me going faster. A friend working about two lines away *saw me bouncing around, as I continued to "pick bones." She started pointing and shouting my name, "Di, Di, Di!"*

In moments, the entire Fillet department started calling my name and pointing. One guy on a lower level took out his phone and started videoing the scene. Of course, the attention inspired me to dance harder, as I enjoyed the movement and the clapping around me. Four hours later, after returning from a short break, the guy who had videoed me dancing stopped me and said, "I didn't know you still had it." Being age 72, many seafood processors were surprised I was there and working as hard as I was. I think they believed someone of my vintage should either be in a rocking chair or dead. I smiled at the guy and, without hesitation, said, "I never lost it!"

Acknowledgments

A sincere thank you to all of my seafood processor friends, who kept me sane and focused during the summer of 2025 in Naknek, Alaska, and encouraged me to write this book. You are all well loved; memories from my "working adventure" continue to make me smile.

Thanks, also, to the friendly staff at the Wilkinson Public Library in Telluride, Colorado. While waiting for the ski season to begin, I spent many days writing this book by a window with a gorgeous view of the mountains.

Finally, thank you to my life partner, Roger Miller, who helped me manage the daunting task of preparing the manuscript for publication. Your support and patience are greatly appreciated.

About the Author

Diane Brady is an award-winning writer and has lived a life of adventure. In Alaska, Diane worked as a journalist, business owner, air taxi pilot, volunteer EMT and FAA Safety Counselor. She served in Belize, C.A. as a U.S. Peace Corps Volunteer (2008-2010). In Colorado, Diane is a Flight Instructor and Personal Trainer. She plans to start building an Experimental, Light-Sport Aircraft in 2026. Diane lives in Durango, Colorado.

www.ingramcontent.com/pod-product-compliance
Lightning Source LLC
Chambersburg PA
CBHW061329120726
48001CB00002B/764